TRACKING TYRANNOSAURS
Meet *T. rex*'s Fascinating Family, from Tiny Terrors to Feathered Giants

BY **CHRISTOPHER SLOAN**   ART BY **XING LIDA** AND **LIU YI**

INTRODUCTION BY **XU XING** AND **PHILIP CURRIE**

NATIONAL GEOGRAPHIC

WASHINGTON, D.C.

Published by the National Geographic Society

John M. Fahey, *Chairman of the Board and Chief Executive Officer*

Declan Moore, *Executive Vice President; President, Publishing and Travel*

Melina Gerosa Bellows, *Executive Vice President; Chief Creative Officer, Books, Kids, and Family*

Prepared by the Book Division

Hector Sierra, *Senior Vice President and General Manager*

Nancy Laties Feresten, *Senior Vice President, Kids Publishing and Media*

Jay Sumner, *Director of Photography, Children's Publishing*

Jennifer Emmett, *Vice President, Editorial Director, Children's Books*

Eva Absher-Schantz, *Design Director, Kids Publishing and Media*

R. Gary Colbert, *Production Director*

Jennifer A. Thornton, *Director of Managing Editorial*

Staff for This Book

Robin Terry, *Project Manager*

Suzanne Patrick Fonda, *Project Editor*

James Hiscott, Jr., *Art Director*

Lori Epstein, *Senior Illustrations Editor*

Ariane Szu-Tu, *Editorial Assistant*

Callie Broaddus, *Design Production Assistant*

Hillary Moloney, *Illustrations Assistant*

Grace Hill, *Associate Managing Editor*

Joan Gossett, *Production Editor*

Lewis R. Bassford, *Production Manager*

Susan Borke, *Legal and Business Affairs*

Manufacturing and Quality Management

Phillip L. Schlosser, *Senior Vice President*

Chris Brown, *Vice President, NG Book Manufacturing*

George Bounelis, *Vice President, Production Services*

Nicole Elliott, *Manager*

Rachel Faulise, *Manager*

Robert L. Barr, *Manager*

This book is for Oliver, Iola, and Leif.

Special thanks are owed to Xu Xing and Philip Currie, whose careful attention to detail has made them great scientists as well as great advisors on this book.

The National Geographic Society is one of the world's largest nonprofit scientific and educational organizations. Founded in 1888 to "increase and diffuse geographic knowledge," the Society's mission is to inspire people to care about the planet. It reaches more than 400 million people worldwide each month through its official journal, *National Geographic*, and other magazines; National Geographic Channel; television documentaries; music; radio; films; books; DVDs; maps; exhibitions; live events; school publishing programs; interactive media; and merchandise. National Geographic has funded more than 10,000 scientific research, conservation, and exploration projects and supports an education program promoting geographic literacy.

For more information, please visit www.nationalgeographic.com, call 1-800-NGS LINE (647-5463), or write to the following address:
National Geographic Society
1145 17th Street N.W.
Washington, D.C. 20036-4688 U.S.A.

Visit us online at www.nationalgeographic.com/books

For librarians and teachers: www.ngchildrensbooks.org

More for kids from National Geographic:
kids.nationalgeographic.com

For information about special discounts for bulk purchases, please contact National Geographic Books Special Sales: ngspecsales@ngs.org

For rights or permissions inquiries, please contact National Geographic Books Subsidiary Rights: ngbookrights@ngs.org

ISBN: 978-1-4263-1374-5 (Trade hardcover)
ISBN: 978-1-4263-1375-2 (Reinforced library binding)

Printed in Hong Kong

13/THK/1

Front cover/title page:
Yutyrannus art by Xing Lida and Liu Yi

CONTENTS

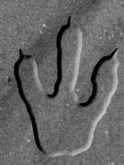

TRACKING TYRANNOSAURS

A WORD FROM TWO WORLD EXPERTS

Looking for tyrannosaurs is hard work. Here a member of an expedition to far western China searches for bones in a desert area where dinosaurs thrived 165 million years ago.

THE TYRANNOSAURS OF CHINA

The word "tyrannosaur" immediately brings to mind images of gigantic dinosaurs with bone-crushing jaws. But new finds reveal a much more varied family tree. Amazing new discoveries in China provide evidence that it was an especially important center for tyrannosaur evolution. So far we have unearthed *Guanlong*, a bizarre-looking Jurassic tyrannosaur with quite a large crest running along the top of its skull, and two others from the early Cretaceous: the small *Dilong* and the gigantic *Yutyrannus*. Combined with discoveries from other parts of the world, these fossils show that the earliest tyrannosaurs of the Jurassic were small with long arms and a great variety of head crests, whereas many head features characterizing gigantic tyrannosaurids appeared in the early Cretaceous—sooner than first thought. Most astonishing of all is the evidence from *Yutyrannus* that even some large tyrannosaurs were covered in long feathers. Through the artwork in the pages ahead you will be able to experience the many different looks of tyrannosaurs throughout their long evolutionary history.

Xu Xing
Institute of Vertebrate Paleontology and Paleoanthropology, Beijing, China

DIGGING IN THE

I started hunting dinosaurs when I was six years old—the plastic kind that came in boxes of cereal. I amassed quite a collection as I ate my way through box after box. The ultimate prize was the terrifying *Tyrannosaurus rex*, but that quest was doomed to failure. Even in cereal boxes, *T. rex* was a rare find. But years later my persistence was rewarded beyond my wildest boyhood expectations. By then I was a professional paleontologist working in the badlands of Alberta, a province in western Canada that is one of the world's richest regions for dinosaur fossils. That's where we discovered not one but two real *T. rex* skeletons! Since then, I have been lucky enough to collect and research the skeletons of many tyrannosaurs in Canada, China, and Mongolia. As you are about to discover, these animals are the most sophisticated killing machines of the entire Age of Dinosaurs. The more tyrannosaurs I find and the more I learn about them, the more awesome they are to me.

Philip Currie
University of Alberta, Edmonton, Canada

WHAT IS A TYRANNOSAUR?

Tyrant lizard king. What sort of creature could live up to that name? Just one: *Tyrannosaurus rex*. This prehistoric giant was one scary dinosaur.

T. rex lived in North America right up to the end of the Age of Dinosaurs. At 40 feet (12 m) long, it was the biggest of all the tyrannosaurs.

The first known fossils of what we now call *Tyrannosaurus rex* were named *Dynamosaurus imperiosus* in 1905.

People waited in line for hours to get a glimpse of *T. rex* in December 1906. That's when the first full skeleton went on display at New York City's American Museum of Natural History. It had taken fossil-hunter Barnum Brown two years to dig out the bones in Montana—the skull alone was reputed to have weighed at least 1,000 pounds (450 kg)—and another two years for museum specialists to put them together. With its huge size and terrifying teeth, this meat-eating giant looked almost as fierce as it did when it roamed North America more than 66 million years ago. It became an instant superstar.

T. rex was found near the end of what has been described as the "Great Dinosaur Rush" of the late 19th century. Fossils of other theropods, or meat-eating dinosaurs, found during this time showed that they had lived 100 million years before *T. rex* and that they were smaller. This evidence made paleontologists think that meat-eating dinosaurs just got bigger and nastier until they reached a maximum size in the form of *T. rex*. Discoveries made over the past two decades show that the evolution of tyrannosaurs is much more complicated.

New "Bone Rush"

There is a lot more variety among tyrannosaurs than was once thought. New discoveries have turned up species with large crests, long snouts, and horny faces. The latest sensation is a feathered giant found in China that some are calling a woolly tyrannosaur! These finds are the result of a new dinosaur "bone rush" in North America and Asia. The evidence clearly shows that tyrannosaurs didn't evolve in a straight line from small to large and that they are more closely related to birds than most other kinds of dinosaurs are.

This drawing of *T. rex* made in 1905 shows how scientists imagined it at the time—a slow, tail-dragging giant. We now know that tyrannosaurs did not drag their tails, but rather used them to balance their bodies over their hips and legs. Strong tail muscles attached to their leg bones helped tyrannosaurs move fast.

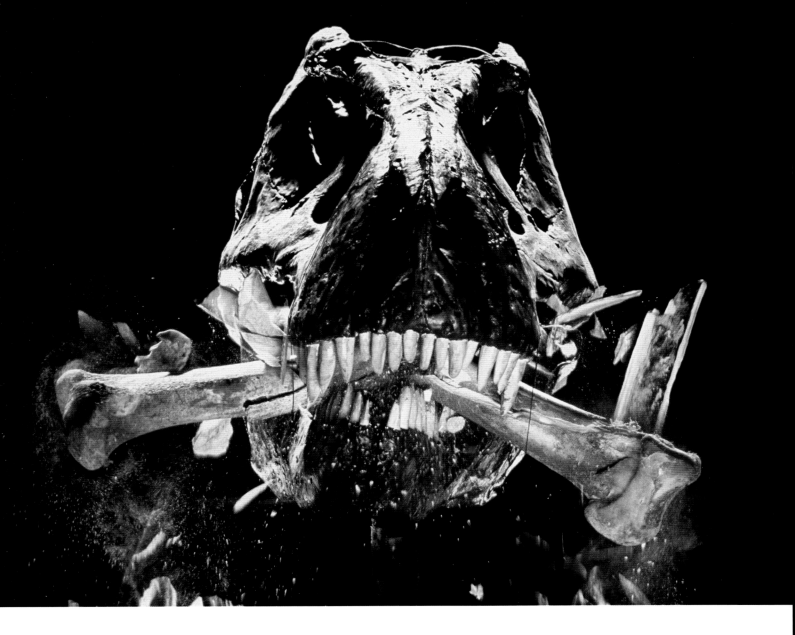

The latest sensation is a FEATHERED GIANT found in CHINA that some are calling a WOOLLY TYRANNOSAUR!

New studies of *T. rex*, including ones that measured the power of its bite, show this dinosaur was a meat-eater that could easily crush big bones into pieces. This photograph shows a model *T. rex* skull smashing an ostrich leg bone as if it were a toothpick.

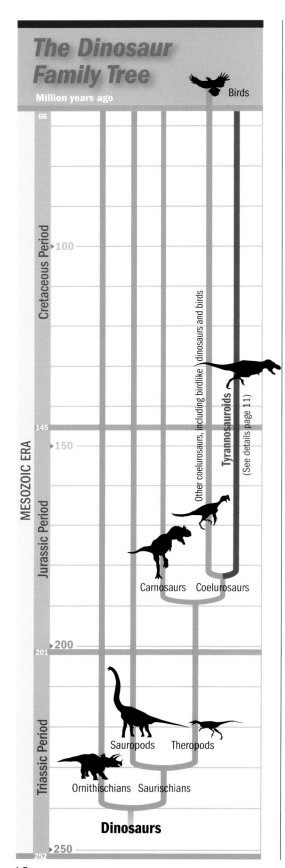

The Dinosaur Family Tree

Million years ago

Birds

Cretaceous Period

100

145

150

MESOZOIC ERA

Jurassic Period

Other coelurosaurs, including birdlike dinosaurs and birds

Tyrannosauroids

(See details page 11)

Carnosaurs   Coelurosaurs

200

201

Triassic Period

Sauropods   Theropods

Ornithischians   Saurischians

Dinosaurs

250

252

The Tyrannosaur-Bird Connection

To say that *T. rex* was an overgrown chicken may not be so far from the truth. What makes tyrannosaurs so closely linked to birds? Like birds they had two legs, walked on three toes, and laid eggs, but so did other kinds of dinosaurs. The best evidence is that like birds, tyrannosaurs had bones laced with air pockets, a wishbone, and feathers. Research shows striking similarities between some *Tyrannosaurus* tissue and that of living birds. Some fossils of *T. rex* even show that it suffered from a fatal disease now found in pigeons.

The Tyrannosaur Family Tree

The overwhelming evidence of a tyrannosaur-bird link that was found in the late 20th century led paleontologists to reclassify tyrannosaurs as coelurosaurs, rather than carnosaurs (see art, left). So even though tyrannosaurs look a lot like carnosaurs, they are now grouped with other birdlike dinosaurs, such as *Oviraptor*, and birds.

What Makes a Tyrannosaur a Tyrannosaur?

A tyrannosaur is any dinosaur that is on the tyrannosauroid branch of the dinosaur family tree (see art, opposite). Scientists use four names when talking about tyrannosaurs. "Tyrannosauroid" is a word used for all tyrannosaurs. "Tyrannosaurid" refers to the giant tyrannosauroids that lived near or at the end of the Cretaceous period, which lasted from 145 to 66 million years ago. Among the tyrannosaurids were "tyrannosaurines," a word used to describe *T. rex* and tyrannosaurs like it, and "albertosaurines," which describes the tyrannosaur *Albertosaurus* and others like it.

The art on pages 12–13 shows some of the features that help scientists identify tyrannosaurs. Generally speaking, the first tyrannosauroids were small, fast predators with long arms and narrow, shallow snouts. They lived in the Jurassic period (201–145 million years ago) and the beginning of the Cretaceous. The tyrannosaurids were mostly giants with big, boxy heads that were wide and deep, powerful jaws, and tiny arms. The tyrannosaur branch of the dinosaur family tree is sure to change as more fossil discoveries are made and new evidence appears. But for now, let's take a look at the tyrannosaurs that have taught us what we know so far.

The Tyrannosaur Family Tree

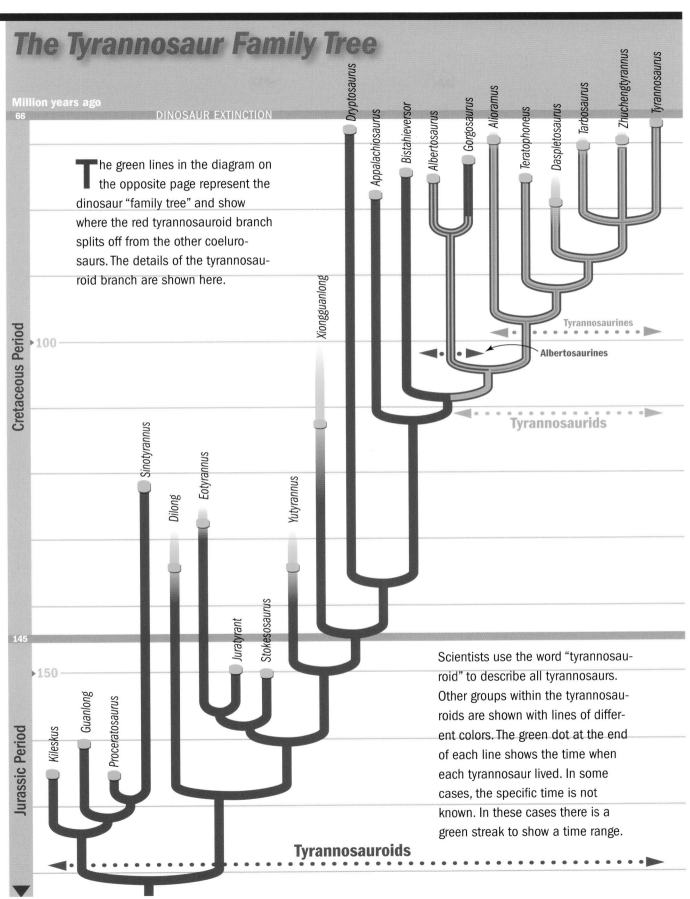

Million years ago

66 — DINOSAUR EXTINCTION

The green lines in the diagram on the opposite page represent the dinosaur "family tree" and show where the red tyrannosauroid branch splits off from the other coelurosaurs. The details of the tyrannosauroid branch are shown here.

Cretaceous Period

100

Jurassic Period

145

150

Tyrannosaurines

Albertosaurines

Tyrannosaurids

Tyrannosauroids

Scientists use the word "tyrannosauroid" to describe all tyrannosaurs. Other groups within the tyrannosauroids are shown with lines of different colors. The green dot at the end of each line shows the time when each tyrannosaur lived. In some cases, the specific time is not known. In these cases there is a green streak to show a time range.

Dryptosaurus
Appalachiosaurus
Bistahieversor
Albertosaurus
Gorgosaurus
Alioramus
Teratophoneus
Daspletosaurus
Tarbosaurus
Zhuchengtyrannus
Tyrannosaurus
Xiongguanlong
Sinotyrannus
Dilong
Eotyrannus
Yutyrannus
Juratyrant
Stokesosaurus
Kileskus
Guanlong
Proceratosaurus

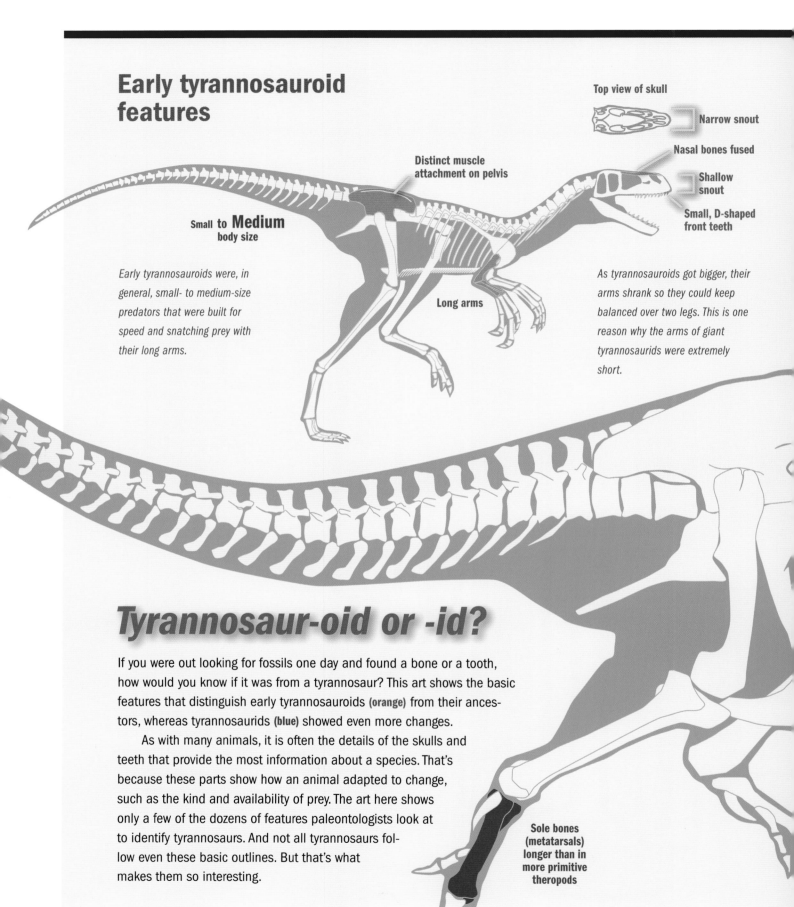

Early tyrannosauroid features

Top view of skull

Narrow snout

Nasal bones fused

Distinct muscle attachment on pelvis

Shallow snout

Small, D-shaped front teeth

Small to Medium body size

Early tyrannosauroids were, in general, small- to medium-size predators that were built for speed and snatching prey with their long arms.

Long arms

As tyrannosauroids got bigger, their arms shrank so they could keep balanced over two legs. This is one reason why the arms of giant tyrannosaurids were extremely short.

Tyrannosaur-oid or -id?

If you were out looking for fossils one day and found a bone or a tooth, how would you know if it was from a tyrannosaur? This art shows the basic features that distinguish early tyrannosauroids **(orange)** from their ancestors, whereas tyrannosaurids **(blue)** showed even more changes.

As with many animals, it is often the details of the skulls and teeth that provide the most information about a species. That's because these parts show how an animal adapted to change, such as the kind and availability of prey. The art here shows only a few of the dozens of features paleontologists look at to identify tyrannosaurs. And not all tyrannosaurs follow even these basic outlines. But that's what makes them so interesting.

Sole bones (metatarsals) longer than in more primitive theropods

Tyrannosaurid features

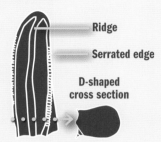

→ Ridge
→ Serrated edge
→ D-shaped cross section

All tyrannosaurs had teeth with serrated, or sawlike, edges, and their front teeth were D-shaped in cross section. In addition, tyrannosaurids had a ridge (see above) along the back of each front tooth.

Top view of tyrannosaurid skull

Big

Wide

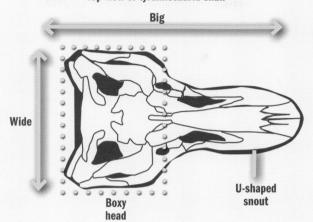

Boxy head

U-shaped snout

Adult tyrannosaurid skulls were big and boxy compared with other tyrannosauroids. But the skulls of young tyrannosaurids (below) were long, narrow, and shallow—just like the skulls of early tyrannosauroids.

Young tyrannosaurid skull

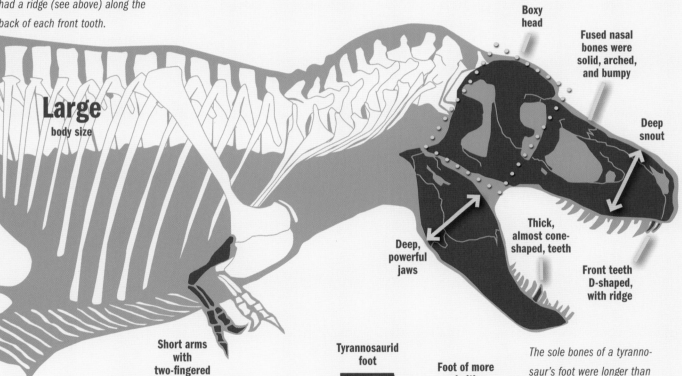

Large body size

Boxy head

Fused nasal bones were solid, arched, and bumpy

Deep snout

Deep, powerful jaws

Thick, almost cone-shaped, teeth

Front teeth D-shaped, with ridge

Short arms with two-fingered hands

Tyrannosaurid foot

Middle sole bone thin at top

Foot of more primitive theropod

The sole bones of a tyrannosaur's foot were longer than those of more primitive theropods. The sole bone that supported the middle toe (red) in tyrannosaurids was thin and spring-like at the top. This adaptation helped them support their heavy bodies and still move quickly.

5 feet

1 meter

CHAPTER TWO

MEET THE TYRANNOSAURS

M ove over *T. rex*. It's time to meet all the other tyrannosaurs to see what they looked like, learn where and when they were found, and find out what they were like when they were alive.

Eotyrannus was an early tyrannosauroid that once lived in what is now the United Kingdom. It was small, but had very large hands for grasping prey.

So far, every tyrannosaur fossil has been found in North America, Asia, or Europe. That's why paleontologists are pretty sure that these meat-eaters evolved on one of the northern continents. The question is, which one?

During the latter part of the Triassic period, which lasted from 252 to 200 million years ago (mya), small theropods lived on many continents, which were then connected as Pangaea (see maps, opposite). Late in the Triassic and early in the Jurassic, however, Europe, Asia, and North America were gradually separated from the southern continents. The earliest known tyrannosaurs appeared about 165 million years ago and were spread across the unconnected northern continents. A common tyrannosauroid ancestor—one that evolved from a small early

Tyrannosaur Dig Sites

Meat-eating dinosaurs evolved during the Triassic period and spread all over the supercontinent Pangaea (see maps, opposite). The earliest known tyrannosaurs spread throughout the northern continents, an area known as Laurasia during the Jurassic. Although there have been claims of finding tyrannosaurs in Australia, the only confirmed discoveries come from the northern continents, as shown by these dig sites.

Russia

United Kingdom
● Juratyrant
Eotyrannus ●● ● Proceratosaurus

EUROPE

ASIA

● Kileskus

Tarbosaurus   Mongolia
Guanlong ● ● ●● ● Alioramus
Xiongguanlong ●

Yutyrannus
●●)) Dilong
Sinotyrannus

China

● Zhuchengtyrannus

AFRICA

INDIAN
OCEAN

AUSTRALIA

● Jurassic tyrannosaurs
● Cretaceous tyrannosaurs
●—● Multiple discoveries of the same species

Jurassic theropod—must have populated the northern continents *before* they broke apart.

No tyrannosaurs are known to have come from Europe after 125 million years ago. The evidence of tyrannosaur evolution after that comes from North America and Asia, which were both connected and disconnected to each other at different times over the rest of the Cretaceous.

To complicate matters, North America was split by a huge inland sea for millions of years, stranding tyrannosaurs on both sides. Dinosaurs on each side of this sea took their own evolutionary paths.

All tyrannosaurs, no matter where they lived, were highly dangerous bundles of muscle, claws, and teeth. This chapter introduces these amazing creatures and what we understand about them today.

U.S.A.
(Alaska)

NORTH
AMERICA

Canada

Gorgosaurus
Albertosaurus
Daspletosaurus

T. rex

Teratophoneus
Stokesosaurus
U.S.A.
Dryptosaurus

Bistahieversor
Appalachiosaurus

PACIFIC
OCEAN

ATLANTIC
OCEAN

EQUATOR

SOUTH
AMERICA

Note: The world map above shows present country boundaries.

TYRANNO*FACT*

The earliest known ancestor of *all* carnivorous dinosaurs, *Eodromaeus*, lived 230 million years ago in South America.

HOW THE CONTINENTS MOVED IN DINOSAUR TIMES

Triassic period: 237 mya

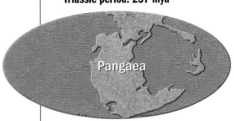

Pangaea

Jurassic period: 170 mya

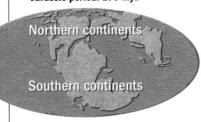

Northern continents

Southern continents

Jurassic period: 152 mya

Laurasia

Gondwana

Cretaceous period: 90 mya

North America Europe Asia

Africa

South America

Australia

Antarctica

GUANLONG

DINO DATABASE

NAME: *Guanlong wucaii*

PRONOUNCED:
(GWAHN-long WOO-sigh)

MEANS:
guan=crown (Chinese)
long=dragon (Chinese)
wucaii=five colors (Chinese)

FOUND IN:
Xinjiang, China

LIVED: 160 mya (Jurassic)

NAME:
Proceratosaurus bradleyi

PRONOUNCED:
(pro-sir-at-oh-SAWR-us
BRAD-lee-eye)

MEANS: pro=before (Latin)
Ceratosaurus=horned dinosaur
(Greek)
bradleyi=named for discoverer
F. Lewis Bradley

FOUND IN: United Kingdom

LIVED: 165 mya (Jurassic)

NAME: *Kileskus aristotocus*

PRONOUNCED:
(kill-ES-kus air-is-TOT-oh-cus)

MEANS: kileskus=lizard (Khakas)
aristotocus=of noble origin (Greek)

FOUND IN: West Siberia, Russia

LIVED: 165 mya (Jurassic)

Two tyrannosaurs fighting to the death, or was one eating the other? Xu Xing and James Clark may never know for sure what happened 160 million years ago at a dig site in what is now northwestern China. What they do know is that in 2002 they discovered a new species of tyrannosaur—one of the earliest ever found. They named it *Guanlong*, which means "crowned dragon" in Chinese. Close examination of the tangle of bones embedded in an 800-pound (360-kg) block of stone revealed not one but two guanlongs of different sizes that had become trapped in mud either while fighting or when one tried to eat the other.

Since the discovery of *Guanlong*, bits and pieces of two other Jurassic tyrannosaurs have surfaced: *Proceratosaurus*, found in England, and *Kileskus*, found in Siberia, Russia (see Dino Database, opposite). Some scientists playfully call these tiny Jurassic terrors "tyrannoraptors" because they were small like the well-known "raptor" dinosaur *Velociraptor*. *Guanlong* was only about 10 feet (3 m) long. It was a fast runner, with longer arms than those of most other tyrannosaurs.

All of these early tyrannosauroids had a thin, boney crest on their snout, but, true to its name, *Guanlong*'s was the largest and most elaborate. The crest was likely used to make showy displays to attract a mate or warn away rivals.

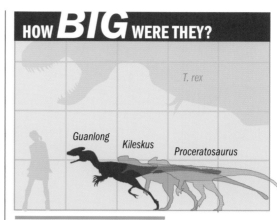

HOW **BIG** WERE THEY?

T. rex

Guanlong *Kileskus* *Proceratosaurus*

1 meter   10 feet

TYRANNOFACT

Tyrannosaurs replaced each tooth about every two years. So that there were never gaps of any more than one tooth in a tyrannosaur jaw, each tooth was replaced at a different time.

Guanlong and other early tyrannosauroids were small, swift predators. *Guanlong* lived in an environment where its prey could have included turtles, small crocs, mammal-like reptiles, and, as this art shows, other guanlongs.

DILONG

DINO DATABASE

NAME: *Dilong paradoxus*

PRONOUNCED: (DEE-long pare-uh-DOX-us)

MEANS: di=emperor (Chinese) long=dragon (Chinese) paradoxus=against received wisdom (Latinized Greek)

FOUND IN: Liaoning Province, China

LIVED: 125 mya (Cretaceous)

NAME: *Eotyrannus lengi*

PRONOUNCED: (EE-oh-tie-RAN-us LENG-eye)

MEANS: eo=dawn (Greek) tyrannus=tyrant (Latin) lengi=named for discoverer Gavin Leng

FOUND IN: United Kingdom

LIVED: 130 to 125 mya (Cretaceous)

NAME: *Juratyrant langhami*

PRONOUNCED: (JOOR-uh-TIE-rant LANG-em-eye)

MEANS: jura=for Jurassic tyrant=tyrant (English) langhami=named for discoverer Peter Langham

FOUND IN: United Kingdom

LIVED: 149 mya (Jurassic)

NAME: *Stokesosaurus clevelandi*

PRONOUNCED: (STOAKS-oh-SAWR-us CLEEVE-land-eye)

MEANS: Stokes=named for discoverer William Lee Stokes saurus=lizard (Greek) clevelandi=for Cleveland, Utah

FOUND IN: Utah, U.S.A.

LIVED: 150 mya (Jurassic)

A feathered tyrannosaur? Most scientists suspected that finding one was just a matter of time. The proof came when *Dilong paradoxus* was found in Liaoning Province in northeastern China in 2004. This was the same place where the first feathered dinosaur—a primitive coelurosaur—was discovered in 1996. Named *Sinosauropteryx*, a name meaning "Chinese dragon feather," it was on the same coelurosaurian branch of the dinosaur family tree as tyrannosaurs. Since it had feathers, there was no reason tyrannosaurs couldn't have had them too. The biggest surprise for scientists was their luck in finding a fossil that preserved imprints of feathers.

HOW *BIG* WERE THEY?

T. rex

Juratyrant

Eotyrannus

Stokesosaurus

Dilong

1 meter

10 feet

Although the *Dilong* find was almost a complete skeleton, the only bits of preserved feathers were found near its head and tail. This led scientists to assume that the body of this small tyrannosaur, which as an adult was only 6.5 feet (2 m) long, was covered in feathers.

The discovery of *Dilong* confirmed that tyrannosaurs could have feathers. Until more feathery fossils are found, however, we won't know which tyrannosaurs had them or what color the feathers were. The art in this book shows what scientists think tyrannosaurs looked like in life.

STEVE BRUSATTE

Dilong is closely related to two other tyrannosauroids that lived in Europe and one from North America (see Dino Database). One of them, *Juratyrant*, was named in 2012 after paleontologist Steve Brusatte took a fresh look at bones in a British museum that were supposed to be from *Stokesosaurus*. They weren't from that dino after all! Both tyrannosaurs were, however, closely related to each other, to *Dilong*, and to *Eotyrannus*, another tyrannosauroid from the U.K.

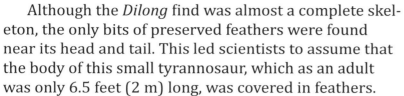

A brightly colored male and a drab female *Dilong* look over their prey, a mammal. Dilongs may have used brightly colored feathers to attract mates.

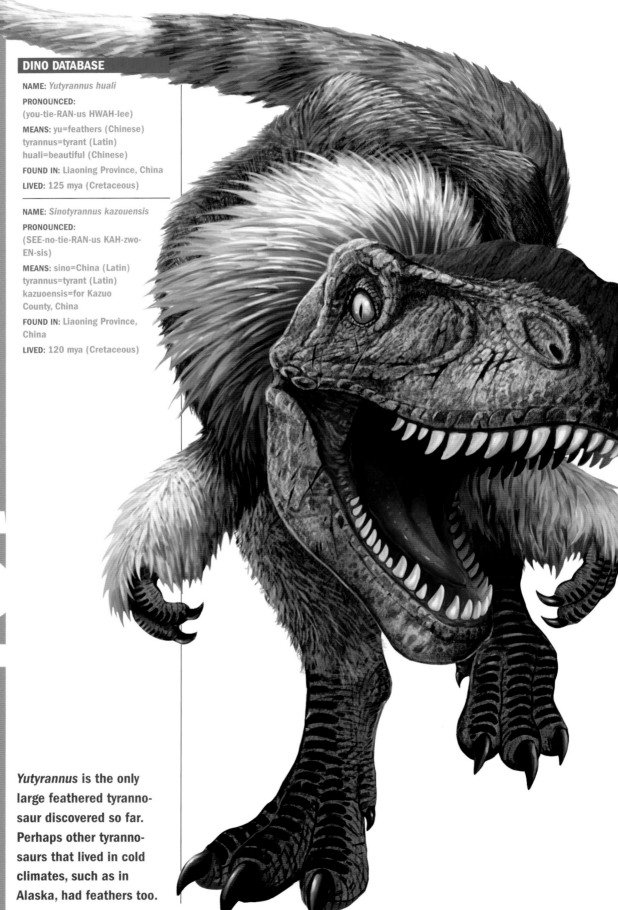

YUTYRANNUS

Yutyrannus **is the only
large feathered tyranno-
saur discovered so far.
Perhaps other tyranno-
saurs that lived in cold
climates, such as in
Alaska, had feathers too.**

22

In 2011 China's Liaoning Province was again making headlines around the world. Three giant feathered tyrannosaurs, named *Yutyrannus*, had been discovered in its famous fossil beds. Finding feathers on small tyrannosaurs like *Dilong* had been almost predictable, but few paleontologists had expected to see them on species 30 feet (9 m) long. Why not? Because feathers, like hair, insulate a body. That is, they keep heat in just like a winter coat does. Large animals generate a lot of internal heat, and they need to get rid of it.

The way furry mammals deal with this is by losing hair as they get larger. Rhinos and elephants are good examples of this. Elephants also shed heat from their large ears. There is one situation in which large mammals keep their hair: a cold environment. The remains of woolly mammoths and woolly rhinos, large animals that survived the cold of many ice ages, show what elephants and rhinos might look like today if they lived in Antarctica.

The long, thick, hairlike feathers, which appeared fossilized in small patches near the neck, hips, and tail of *Yutyrannus,* were up to eight inches (20 cm) long. This showed that it was probably covered from head to tip of tail with feathers. Paleontologists wondered what a large tyrannosaur was doing with so many feathers. Didn't it need to lose heat?

When *Yutyrannus* lived in the early part of the Cretaceous, the average temperature in northeastern China was 14°F (8°C) cooler than later in the Cretaceous, the toasty time when *T. rex* lived. It may be that *Yutyrannus* was a "woolly" tyrannosaur that used its feathers to keep warm.

XU XING

When new feathered dinosaurs are found in China, Xu Xing is often the first person called. The fossils are found by farmers or other workers and reported to local museums. When Xu first saw *Yutyrannus* in 2009, it looked like it could be *Sinotyrannus*, a 30- to 33-foot (9- to 10-m)-long tyrannosauroid that had already been named in 2009 (see Dino Database). Yet the *Sinotyrannus* fossil had no sign of feathers. Closer inspection showed Xu that he was looking at a new kind of dinosaur. *Sinotyrannus* lived in what is now China only about five million years after *Yutyrannus*. Could *Sinotyrannus* have been another feathered giant?

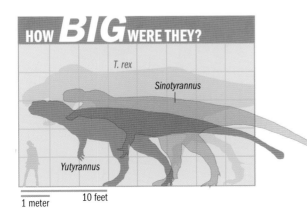

HOW *BIG* WERE THEY?

T. rex

Sinotyrannus

Yutyrannus

1 meter   10 feet

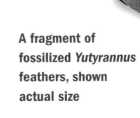

A fragment of fossilized *Yutyrannus* feathers, shown actual size

If any tyrannosaur can be considered a link between the small-bodied early tyrannosauroids and the much larger tyrannosaurids that lived at the end of the Cretaceous it would be *Xiongguanlong*. Named in 2009, *Xiongguanlong* was a medium-size tyrannosauroid, weighing in at 600 pounds (270 kg)—about the weight of a male grizzly bear. It lived right in the middle of what was a 40-million-year-long blank spot in tyrannosaur history. Its discovery provided scientists with a rare look at how tyrannosaurids evolved during that time. Even though it was smaller,

DINO DATABASE

NAME: *Xiongguanlong baimoensis*

PRONOUNCED:
(SHEEONG-gwahn-long
BY-moh-EN-sis)

MEANS:
Xiong Guan=Grand Pass (Chinese)
long=dragon (Chinese)
baimo=white ghost (Chinese)
ensis=from (Latin)

FOUND IN: Gansu Province, China

LIVED: 125 to 100 mya (Cretaceous)

Xiongguanlong had some hallmark traits of the giant tyrannosaurids. It had a boxy head and D-shaped front teeth, with a ridge running down the back of each. *Xiongguanlong* also had boney ridges over its eyes, as did *T. rex* and other later Cretaceous giants.

In addition to its tyrannosaurid traits, however, *Xiongguanlong* shared traits with earlier tyrannosauroids, such as its long, shallow snout and teeth that were flattened rather than cone-shaped.

Why were tyrannosaurs changing? The best explanation may be that the new traits were related to shifting eating and feeding behavior. A boxier head supported more-massive jaws with thicker muscles, and that made more powerful bites possible. With a snout two-thirds the length of its skull, however, *Xiongguanlong* was not well-suited for crunching bones.

Even though *Xiongguanlong*'s snout was long, its nose bones, or nasals, were solid and not full of air spaces like those of *Dilong*. This means that while *Xiongguanlong* probably didn't have a powerful bite, its snout hinted at the solid, arched nasals that helped make the giant tyrannosaurids such bone crunchers.

Ridge

1 millimeter

Although it was a medium-size tyrannosauroid, *Xiongguanlong* shows that heads were getting bigger in the tyrannosaur lineage. It had one of the longest snouts among the tyrannosaurs.

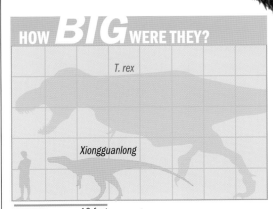

HOW **BIG** WERE THEY?

T. rex

Xiongguanlong

1 meter   10 feet

25

TYRANNOFACT

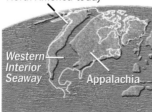

Shorelines of
North America today

Western
Interior
Seaway

Appalachia

Tyrannosauroids living on Appalachia never evolved into tyrannosaurids.

The story of tyrannosaur evolution in North America is complicated by a major change in the continent's geography during the Cretaceous. Shifting continental plates and rising sea levels caused a vast sea to drown much of the area between the Rocky Mountains and the Mississippi River all the way from the Arctic Ocean to the Gulf of Mexico (see Tyrannofact). As a result, dinosaurs that were stranded on either side of what scientists call the Western Interior Seaway followed different evolutionary paths. The sea gradually disappeared, but not until after most dinosaurs went extinct 66 million years ago. Species on either side of the sea—including tyrannosaurs—evolved separately for 35 million years!

So far, scientists have discovered only two tyrannosaurs that were stranded on the landmass to the east of the sea, an area scientists call Appalachia. These were *Dryptosaurus* and *Appalachiosaurus*.

Dryptosaurus was one of the first dinosaurs discovered in North America. Stoneworkers found its skeleton in a New Jersey quarry in 1866. Edward Cope, an American paleontologist famous for studying fossils found as the American West was explored in the 19th century, knew these bones were from a fierce predator. This medium-size dinosaur had sharp teeth and large hands with big, curved claws, which reminded Cope of eagle talons.

Paleontologists did not find the other "Appalachian" tyrannosaur until 1982, this time in Alabama. Unlike *Dryptosaurus*, which was found in pieces, this discovery was a well-preserved skeleton. They named it *Appalachiosaurus*.

Scientists were at first challenged to find a place for *Dryptosaurus* and *Appalachiosaurus* on the dinosaur

Unlike tyrannosaurids in western North America, *Dryptosaurus* had long arms and unusually long, talon-like claws that were useful for hunting prey, such as the prehistoric croc behind this rock.

family tree. Tyrannosaur discoveries since 1982, however, have made the picture a bit more clear. We now know that tyrannosaurs on both sides of the sea may have evolved from a common *Xiongguanlong*-like ancestor. But once the eastern and western parts of North America were separated, the tyrannosaurs stranded on either side evolved very differently.

While tyrannosauroids in Appalachia kept basic tyrannosauroid features, those in the west changed dramatically over time. *Bistahieversor,* a tyrannosauroid recently discovered in New Mexico (see Dino Database), shows early signs of these changes. At 30 feet (9 m) long, *Bistahieversor* is the first tyrannosauroid with the sort of big jaws seen later in tyrannosaurids like *T. rex.*

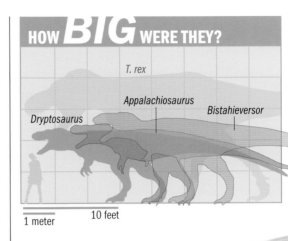

HOW **BIG** WERE THEY?

T. rex

Appalachiosaurus

Dryptosaurus

Bistahieversor

1 meter   10 feet

DINO DATABASE

NAME: *Albertosaurus sarcophagus*

PRONOUNCED: (al-BER-toh-SAWR-us sahr-COUGH-uh-gus)

MEANS: alberto=named for Alberta, Canada
saurus=lizard (Greek)
sarcophagus=flesh-eating (Greek)

FOUND IN: Alberta, Canada

LIVED: 73 mya (Cretaceous)

NAME: *Gorgosaurus libratus*

PRONOUNCED: (gor-goh-SAWR-us lib-RAH-tus)

MEANS: gorgo=terrible, fierce (Greek)
saurus=lizard (Greek)
libratus=weigh, balance (Latin)

FOUND IN: Alberta, Canada

LIVED: 75 mya (Cretaceous)

NAME: *Daspletosaurus torosus*

PRONOUNCED: (das-PLEET-oh-SAWR-us toh-ROW-sus)

MEANS: daspleto=frightful (Greek)
saurus=lizard (Greek)
torosus=muscular (Latin)

FOUND IN: Alberta, Canada

LIVED: 83 to 75 mya (Cretaceous)

NAME: *Teratophoneus curriei*

PRONOUNCED: (teh-RAT-oh-PHONE-ee-us CUR-ee-eye)

MEANS: terato=monster (Greek)
phoneus=murderer (Greek)
curriei=named for paleontologist Philip Currie

FOUND IN: Utah, U.S.A.

LIVED: 76 mya (Cretaceous)

Being chased by one tyrannosaur would be bad enough, but imagine being hunted by a pack. That's the possibility Philip Currie discovered when he and his team dug up a 72-million-year-old bone bed in Canada filled with 22 albertosaurs.

Albertosaurus was one of five known tyrannosaurids—the giant tyrannosaurs that dominated western North America late in the Cretaceous period. Three of them—*Albertosaurus, Gorgosaurus,* and *Daspletosaurus*—are known only from remains found in western Canada (see Dino Database). *Tyrannosaurus rex,* known from the United States and Canada, and *Teratophoneus,*

a short-snouted tyrannosaur from Utah that is also the earliest known tyrannosaurid, are the other two.

Although not as large as *T. rex*, the Canadian tyrannosaurids were truly giants—weighing in between 1,300 to more than 3,000 pounds (600 to 1,360 kg) as adults and measuring up to 30 feet (9 m) long. Their heads and jaws were even boxier and stronger than *Bistahieversor*'s. Their arms were very small and had two fingers instead of three. A U-shaped row of long, strong teeth made their jaws ideal for ripping and pulling at flesh.

While the three Canadian dinosaurs look very similar, *Albertosaurus* and *Gorgosaurus* are more lightly built than *Daspletosaurus* and *Teratophoneus*. That is why *Albertosaurus* and *Gorgosaurus* are called albertosaurines, while *Daspletosaurus* and *Teratophoneus* are tyrannosaurines—just like *Tyrannosaurus rex*.

TYRANNOSAUR TRACKER

PHILIP CURRIE

Philip Currie spent much of his career digging up dinosaurs in Alberta, Canada. That's where he found 22 albertosaurs at Dry Island Buffalo Jump Provincial Park. The fossils gave Currie a rare chance to study a large group of tyrannosaurs that had lived— and died—together in the same environment. Since albertosaurs of all ages, including a two-year-old and a very old 33-foot (10-m)-long one, lived together, Currie suggests they likely hunted together.

The fossil skeletons of different-aged albertosaurs were found together in Alberta, Canada. One rare find was an albertosaur that was just two years old.

HOW BIG WERE THEY?

T. rex
Albertosaurus   Gorgosaurus   Daspletosaurus
Teratophoneus

1 meter   10 feet

TARBOSAURUS

NAME: *Tarbosaurus bataar*

PRONOUNCED: (tar-boh-SAWR-us bah-TAR)

MEANS: **tarbo=alarm, dread, terror (Greek)**
saurus=lizard (Greek)
bataar=misspelling of "baatar," meaning "hero" (Mongolian)

FOUND IN: **Mongolia**

LIVED: **71 to 68 mya (Cretaceous)**

NAME: *Zhuchengtyrannus magnus*

PRONOUNCED: (joo-chung teh-RAN-us MAG-nus)

MEANS: **zhucheng=named for Zhucheng, China**
tyrannus=tyrant (Latin)
magnus=great (Latin)

FOUND IN: **Zhucheng, China**

LIVED: **72 to 69 mya (Cretaceous)**

North America was not the only place giant tyrannosaurids lived late in the Cretaceous. Megapredators stalked parts of Asia as well. One of these was *Tarbosaurus*, found in Mongolia in the 1940s. It was close to *T. rex* in size, but *Tarbosaurus* had a longer, more narrow head and the muscles it used to control its bite were arranged differently. These features may have evolved in response to different food choices from those available to *T. rex*, such as armor-plated ankylosaurs instead of horned and frilled triceratops. The foot of *Tarbosaurus,* with its middle toe bone thin at the top, was very similar to *T. rex*'s foot and shows that the two giants carried their weight the same way.

For many years *Tarbosaurus* was the only known

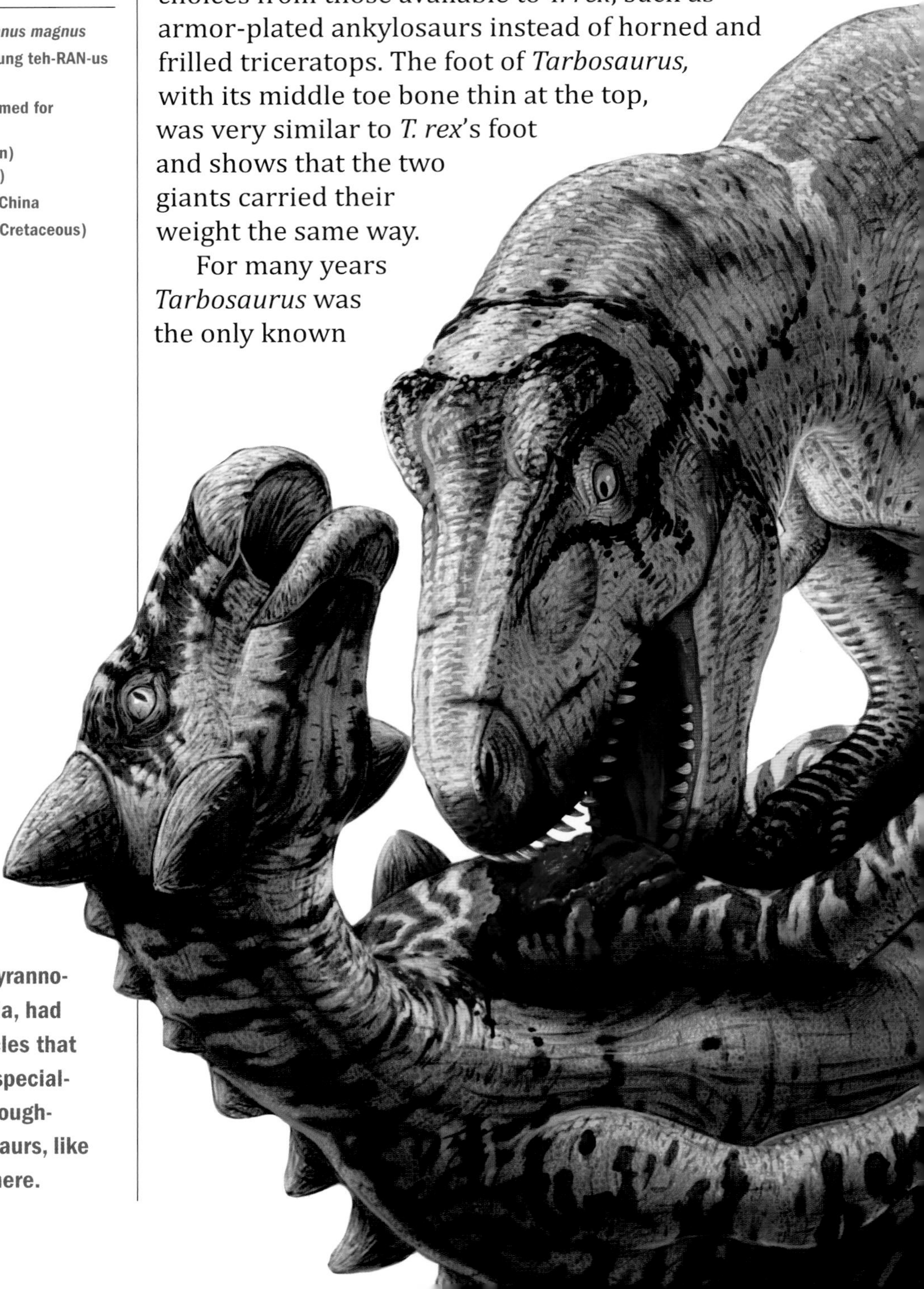

Tarbosaurus, a tyrannosaurine from Asia, had strong jaw muscles that may have been specialized for eating tough-skinned ankylosaurs, like the one shown here.

tyrannosaur from Asia that got anywhere near the size of *T. rex*. Then in the 1970s near the city of Zhucheng in Shandong Province, China, some *T. rex*-like teeth were discovered among the bones of duck-billed dinosaurs. It was not until 2009, however, that pieces of upper and lower jaw bones were found at the same site. That's when scientists knew they had found another Asian giant that lived at the same time as *Tarbosaurus*. They named it *Zhuchengtyrannus magnus* (see Dino Database). With only small differences in their skulls, both *Tarbosaurus* and *Zhuchengtyrannus* are very similar to *T. rex*. Scientists call them both tyrannosaurines.

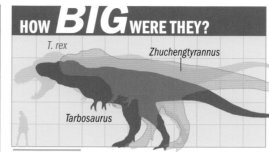

HOW *BIG* WERE THEY?

T. rex
Zhuchengtyrannus
Tarbosaurus

1 meter   10 feet

TYRANNOFACT

A recent study of a young *Tarbosaurus* skull showed that it could easily be mistaken for a more primitive species of tyrannosauroid. This suggests that identifying new tyrannosaur species based on young specimens can be tricky business.

ALIORAMUS

DINO DATABASE

NAME: *Alioramus altai*

PRONOUNCED: (al-ee-oh-RAY-mus ALL-tie)

MEANS: alio=other (Latin)
ramus=branch (Latin)
altai=named for the Altai Mountains

FOUND IN: Mongolia

LIVED: 71 to 68 mya (Cretaceous)

In 1976 a team of Russian and Mongolian scientists made a bizarre discovery in the Gobi: a tyrannosaur with a distinctly different look. It was not a giant, and its skull was shallow and narrow, more like that of *Xiongguanlong*. They called it *Alioramus*.

Because the fossil was badly preserved, *Alioramus*'s relationship to other tyrannosaurs was not clear. Some scientists even thought it was a young *Tarbosaurus*. But in 2009, scientists announced the discovery of another *Alioramus*. This time the fossil was in great shape. Although *Alioramus* was a very unusual tyrannosaurine, it clearly was closely related to *Tarbosaurus*.

Alioramus's body was not bulky and muscular like the other tyrannosaurines. It was sleek and built for speed. The dino's skull was also so full of air spaces that it was lighter than any other known tyrannosaurine. This suggests *Alioramus* had habits very different from those of the giant *Tarbosaurus*, which lived at the same time and same place.

A most unusual feature of *Alioramus* were the eight bumps on its skull, which in life would have looked like small horns. These

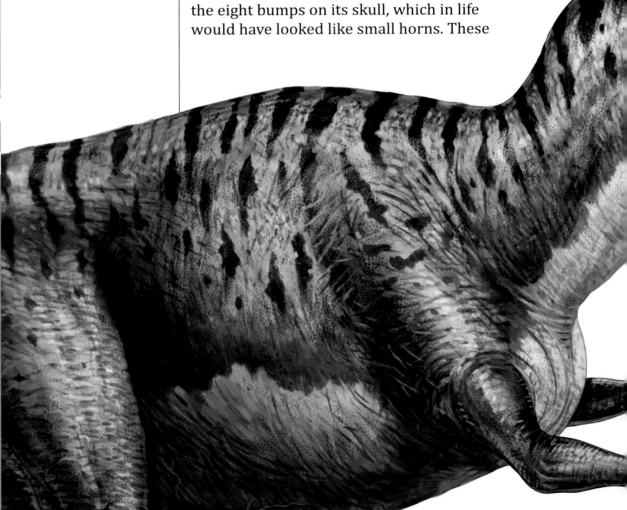

appeared on its snout, above its eyes, and on its cheekbones. Although some other tyrannosaurs had crests on their noses and ridges above their eyes, no other tyrannosaur was as oddly ornamented as *Alioramus*. It is possible these ornaments were used to compete for mates.

The exact relationship between Asian and North American tyrannosaurines is not clear. Most evidence shows that *Alioramus* and *Tarbosaurus* were more closely related to each other than to their North American cousins. This suggests that the Asian tyrannosaurines evolved independently despite the fact that land bridges provided a way for creatures to travel between Asia and North America at different points during the Cretaceous.

TYRANNOSAUR TRACKER

MARK NORELL

The Gobi is a special place for paleontologist Mark Norell. He has spent many summers looking for dinosaurs in extremely remote regions, traveling by truck convoys that carry all the food, water, and supplies for the months-long digs. In 2001 his team discovered the bones of the first *Alioramus* found since the Mongolian-Russian discovery in 1976. It was about half the size of an adult *Tarbosaurus* that had just been found in the same spot. The differences between the two tyrannosaurines probably made it possible for them to live in the same place without too much direct competition for food.

Alioramus was unusual for a tyrannosaurine. Weighing about 800 pounds (360 kg), its body was smaller than other known close relatives of *T. rex*, and its snout was covered with small horns.

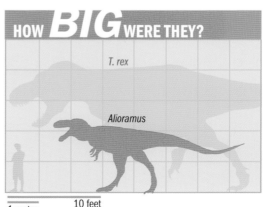

HOW **BIG** WERE THEY?

T. rex

Alioramus

1 meter   10 feet

One of *T. rex's* food sources was *Triceratops*, a gigantic plant-eater with sharp horns and a thick, boney frill to protect its neck. *T. rex* tooth marks have been found in their frills.

Everything about *T. rex* prepared it for maximum bone-crushing action. Its powerful jaws and large serrated teeth could rip off up to 500 pounds (225 kg) of meat in one bite. It didn't have to worry about bones. They just got chewed up with the meat.

Tyrannosaurus rex is the only known tyrannosaurine that lived right up to the end of the Cretaceous period 66 million years ago. It was truly a giant, standing 15 feet (4.6 m) tall, 40 feet (12 m) long, and weighing as much as 16,000 pounds (7,250 kg). Its huge 5-foot (1.5-m)-long head was balanced by a massive 25-foot (7.6-m)-long tail.

The discovery of other giant prehistoric predators, such as *Spinosaurus* and *Cacharadontosaurus* from Africa and *Giganotosaurus* from South America, robbed *T. rex* of its long-held title as largest meat-eater. But it is definitely the largest coelurosaur.

Although *T. rex* fossils have been found all over western North America, more than two dozen of the most complete and best preserved come from the Hell Creek formation that extends through Montana, North Dakota, and South Dakota. Microscopic examination of these bones has made it possible for scientists to discover growth lines that help determine not only the age of a *Tyrannosaurus* when it died but also how fast it grew. Soft tissue that has not fully turned to stone has been found inside some *T. rex* bones from Montana. One type that is being studied is collagen, a protein that helps form bone. Scientists see similarities in collagen found in *T. rex* and collagen found in birds. This shows just how closely related birds and tyrannosaurs are.

HOW *BIG* WERE THEY?

Tyrannosaurus rex

1 meter   10 feet

TYRANNOSAUR TRACKER

JOHN "JACK" HORNER

John Horner grew up in Montana and found his first fossil when he was a young boy. Since then, he has spent decades digging in the Hell Creek formation to learn more about the world of tyrannosaurs. Many *T. rexes* have been found by Horner's team. These have helped flesh out a picture of *T. rex* as a living, breathing animal. Just as important, however, are the thousands of fossils of other animals and plants found in the Hell Creek formation. They help us understand the environment that was *T. rex*'s world.

CHAPTER THREE

REVEALING TYRANNOSAUR SECRETS

Thanks to scientists who travel the world to track down tyrannosaur fossils and to the high-tech tools they use to study their finds, we can better understand how these creatures moved, hunted, ate, fought, and more.

Using new tools and new finds, scientists will be able to answer questions we still have about tyrannosaurs, such as what kind of parents they were. Here, a grown-up *Appalachiosaurus* encounters a hatchling.

TYRANNO*FACT*

Being a giant tyrannosaur was a balancing act. As their heads became huge and heavy, their arms became puny as a way of keeping their bodies in balance with their tails.

Paleontologists have discovered a lot of *Albertosaurus sarcophagus* and *T. rex* fossils, which is why many studies of tyrannosaur biology and possible behavior are based on these two species. To get a more complete view of the past, dozens of expeditions search every year for more bones.

Digging Up Dinosaurs

Understanding tyrannosaurs involves more than just looking for bones. Finding other dinosaurs as well as plants, mammals, insects, and other creatures that lived around them creates a picture of their ancient environment. This is called fieldwork. It also means understanding natural events, such as volcanic eruptions, droughts, and floods, that might have caused the death of prehistoric plants and animals at a site.

Boney Details

A museum or university laboratory is where the tedious task of preparing a specimen for study is done. Starting with a block of stone containing fossil bones, technicians use what looks and sounds like a dentist's drill to clean away material that is not bone. Then scientists can measure the bones and note their different sizes and shapes. These details can show what species of tyrannosaur the bones belonged to, how large it was, and how much it weighed. Bones can also reveal signs of fighting, disease, or feeding behavior. One tyrannosaur meal was a *Triceratops*. Its pelvis shows it was chomped on, leaving behind 58 tyrannosaur tooth marks.

Some fossils show that tyrannosaurs were not only biting other

Once fossils arrive in a laboratory, the bones are carefully teased out of the rock by experts. It can take hundreds of hours of detailed work to get a specimen ready for study.

One tyrannosaur MEAL was a Triceratops. Its pelvis shows it was CHOMPED ON, leaving behind 58 tyrannosaur TOOTH MARKS.

Every year fossil bones erode out of the ground naturally. This doesn't mean they're easy to find or collect. Sometimes only a small bit has been exposed. Fossils are often either very fragile or embedded in very hard stone. This makes for what can be very hard work. In this picture a few dinosaur bones, and some broken bits, are visible in the center of the image.

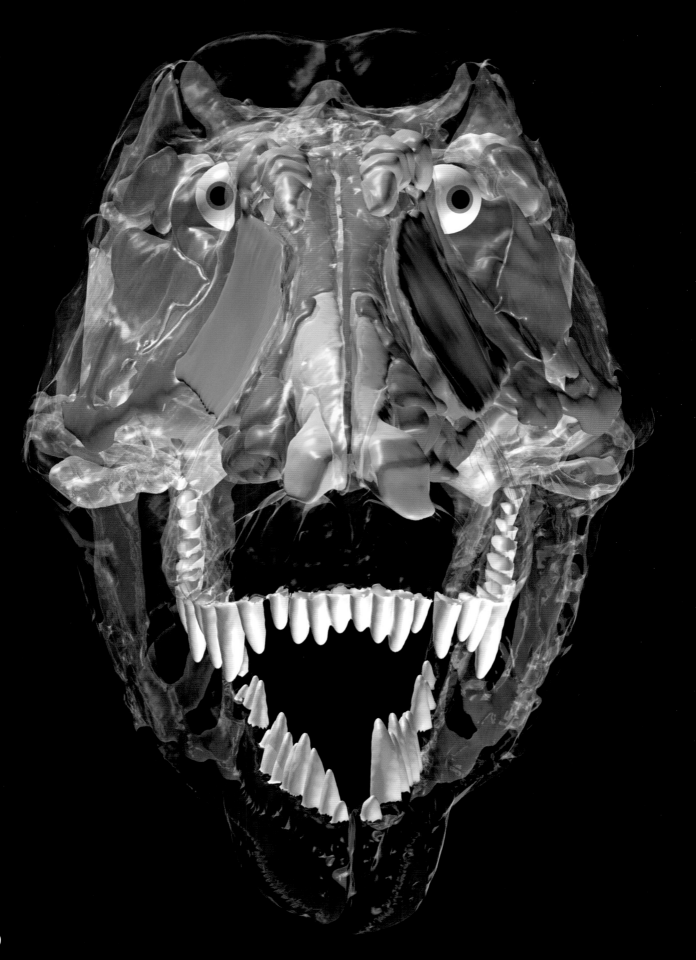

dinosaurs but also each other. Fossilized bite marks on snouts and feet may have been suffered in battles for food or mates. Other bite marks may be evidence of cannibalism.

Bone Secrets

Dinosaur bones, like tree trunks, create rings as they grow. To view these rings, scientists shave thin cross sections from fossil bones. Then by counting the rings and measuring the spaces between them, scientists can tell how old a tyrannosaur was when it died and how fast it was growing at different ages. Recent studies combined this information with estimates of a tyrannosaur's weight at different ages to show that North American tyrannosaurids grew fastest between the ages of 10 and 20 years. After the age of 20 or so they stopped growing. Similar studies show that *T. rex* packed on between 1,690 and 3,950 pounds (770 and 1,790 kg) each year during its teen years in order to reach its adult size by age 20.

CT Scanning

Another way to look inside bones is with computed tomography (CT) scanning. One study revealed that a *T. rex* snout contained complex spiraling structures that would have greatly expanded its smelling surface. Another study that used CT scanning to peer inside a *T. rex* head showed an enlarged olfactory lobe, the part of the brain devoted to

In 1988 scientists restudied the fossil of a small tyrannosaur found in 1942. They decided it was a new kind and named it *Nanotyrannus*. Research on new fossil finds revealed how much change tyrannosaurs go through as they mature. Many experts now think *Nanotyrannus* is really a young *T. rex*.

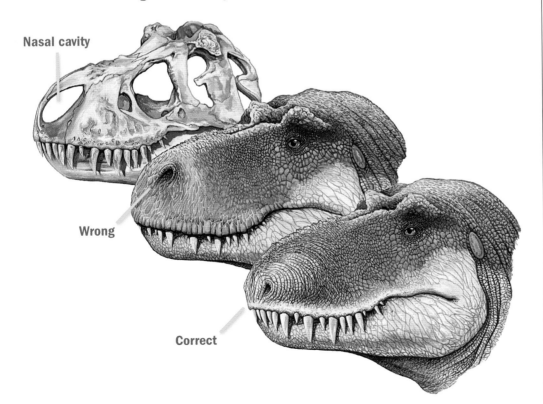

Nasal cavity

Wrong

Correct

Scanning the fossil skull of a *T. rex* revealed that its head was filled with large spaces called sinuses (shown in color, opposite) that made the skull lighter and stronger. Studies that compared a *T. rex* skull with those of birds and reptiles showed that artists have been putting the tyrant king's nostrils in the wrong place for years. They should be at the front of the nose, as shown at left.

An *Albertosaurus* is spooked by a lunging *Deinosuchus*. Recent studies have shown that while tyrannosaurs had bone-crunching bites, they did not match the power of giant crocs like *Deinosuchus*.

Even if a T. REX were RUNNING at 25 miles an hour, it would still BEAT the FASTEST HUMAN in a 100-meter dash.

smell. These finds are strong evidence that *T. rex* could smell better than any other meat-eating dinosaur.

Bite Power

The jaws of *T. rex* were among the most powerful ever to evolve. But just how powerful they were and how their skull was able to withstand the stress of breaking through bone are questions of special interest to scientists.

The strength of skulls can be measured with the same tools that engineers use to test stress on airplanes and bridges. These tests show that the skulls of tyrannosaurids were reinforced to withstand great forces. Structures like their fused and arched nasal bones contributed to this strength.

Bite force can be measured with a pressure-sensing device. Since there are no living tyrannosaurs to test, scientists use alligators and crocodiles instead and scale the results according to the size of the dinosaur being studied.

Computer Modeling

To answer questions like "How fast could *T. rex* run?," scientists turn to computer modeling and to biomechanics, which is the science of how living things move. Since dinosaurs are no longer living, scientists create computer model dinosaurs based on their bones and estimates of how much muscle and body weight they carried. That's why different studies produce slightly different answers. One calculated *T. rex*'s speed between 10 and 25 miles per hour (16 and 40 kph); another clocked its speed at about 29 miles per hour (47 kph). Whichever is true, it is a

TYRANNOFACT

The eye sockets of *T. rex* faced forward, giving the dinosaur the ability to focus both eyes on an object at the same time. This made it possible for *T. rex* to figure out how near or far its prey was.

All tyrannosaur teeth had saw-like edges and could cut easily through skin and flesh. The teeth of tyrannosaurids (left) were still saw-edged, but were shaped more like cones than the teeth of earlier tyrannosauroids, giving them more crunching power.

The preservation of *Sinosauropteryx* (right) was so good that the dinosaur's feather color could be determined. Scientists can probably thank rapid burial in mud and volcanic ash for preserving imprints of the feathers of *Dilong* (opposite).

good thing *T. rex* is extinct. The average top speed of the world's fastest human is 23 miles per hour (37 kph). Even if a *T. rex* were running at 25 miles an hour, it would still beat the fastest human in a 100-meter dash.

Dino DNA?

Using techniques from microbiology and genetics laboratories as well as powerful microscopes, scientists are studying the structure of dinosaur bone, skin, and feathers, as well as rare samples of soft tissue found in those bones.

These studies show that it is possible to identify collagen, a protein found in bone and other body tissue, in the bones of dinosaurs. Another study identified medullary bone in the hollow leg bone of a *T. rex*. Medullary bone forms in egg-laying birds and helps store calcium for eggshells. The fossilized medullary was identical to that seen in the bones of pregnant female birds. The *T. rex* was about to lay eggs! This was the first time a tyrannosaur had been positively identified as male or female.

In 2010 scientists found organic material called melanosomes preserved in the feathers of *Sinosauropteryx* that were identical to what appears in the feathers of living birds. Melanosomes are pigment-filled structures of different shapes. Different colors are produced depending on their shape and how the melanosomes are arranged in a feather. Fossil melanosomes helped scientists figure out the colors of this primitive coelurosaur's feathery coat: rust orange and white.

The feathers of *Yutyrannus* and *Dilong* have been checked, but they have not yet provided color information. Perhaps some day a paleontologist will discover feathers on other tyrannosaurs—maybe even *T. rex*!

Could someone piece together a genetic map of a tyrannosaur from preserved organic material and use it to clone a dinosaur? It's a challenge so difficult, it's close to being science fiction. But science has a way of solving problems that seem impossible to us today. Sooner or later, someone will probably discover exactly how to turn a chicken into a tyrannosaur. Will it be you?

GLOSSARY

albertosaurine
An albertosaurine is a member of the subfamily Albertosaurinae. Animals from this group have been discovered in northwestern North America but not in Asia.

ankylosaur
An ankylosaur is a member of a group of plant-eating dinosaurs covered in boney plates. They were widespread and have been found on every continent except Africa.

biomechanics
Biomechanics is a field of study that uses the principles of mechanics to learn how animals move.

carnivore/carnivorous
"Carnivore" comes from the Latin words *carne* meaning "flesh" and *vorare* meaning "to devour." Carnivores are animals that eat almost entirely animal flesh.

carnosaur
A carnosaur is a member of a group of large, meat-eating theropod dinosaurs more primitive than coelurosaurs.

ceratopsian
A ceratopsian is a member of a group of plant-eating dinosaurs that includes horned animals such as *Triceratops*. The main trait of ceratopsians is a parrot-like beak.

coelurosaur
A coelurosaur is a member of a group of theropods considered to be closely related to birds. Many coelurosaurs have feathers, and the group includes living birds.

collagen
Collagen is a protein commonly found in the flesh, bone, and connective tissue of vertebrates.

computed tomography (CT)
Computed tomography is an imaging process that uses x-rays to see inside objects and produce cross sections, or "slices," of specific areas.

computer modeling
Computer modeling involves using a computer to understand processes and interactions and to test different ideas.

Cretaceous period
The Cretaceous period lasted from 145 to 66 million years ago. During this time Earth was warmer and wetter and covered by large seas.

fossil
A fossil is the remains of an animal, plant, or other living thing from the distant past. Fossilization takes place when living tissue is replaced by inorganic minerals, turning it to stone.

genetics
Genetics is the science of examining how genes, the parts of DNA that control inherited characteristics, are transferred from one living organism to its descendants.

Gondwana
Gondwana is the name for an ancient landmass that existed before about 180 million years ago. It included the southern continents, the Arabian Peninsula, and the Indian subcontinent.

Jurassic period
The Jurassic period lasted from 201 to 145 million years ago.

Laurasia
Laurasia is the name for an ancient landmass that existed before about 180 million years ago. It included North America, Europe, and Asia.

melanosome
A melanosome is a structure within a cell that contains melanin, a light-absorbing pigment.

Mesozoic era
The Mesozoic era lasted from 250 million years ago to 66 million years ago. Because this was the time when dinosaurs thrived, it is often called the Age of Dinosaurs.

microbiology
Microbiology is the study of microscopic organisms.

mya
Mya is an abbreviation for "million years ago."

olfactory lobe
The olfactory lobe is a section of the brain used to sense odor.

ornithischian
An ornithischian is a member of Ornithischia, one of the two main groups of dinosaurs. Ornithischians are plant-eaters identified by having a bone in the hip, called the pubis, that points backward.

Oviraptor
Oviraptor is a small meat-eating, bird-like coelurosaur.

paleontologist
A paleontologist studies paleontology, the scientific study of prehistoric life that relies on fossils and data about past environments to determine what prehistoric life was like and how it evolved over time.

Pangaea
Pangaea is the name for a supercontinent that included all modern continents. It formed about 300 million years ago and split up around 200 million years ago.

saurischian
A saurischian is a member of Saurischia, one of the two main groups of dinosaurs. Saurischians include all the carnivorous dinosaurs and the long-necked plant-eaters called sauropods, among others.

sauropod
A sauropod is a member of a subgroup of saurischian dinosaurs known for having very long necks and tails and thick, stocky legs.

theropod
A theropod is a member of a subgroup of saurischian dinosaurs called Theropoda. All theropods walked on two feet and most were carnivorous. There were many kinds of theropods, including carnosaurs and coelurosaurs, but birds are the only theropods alive today.

Triassic period
The Triassic period lasted from about 252 to 201 million years ago. At the beginning and end of the Triassic period there were extinction events that wiped out many kinds of plants and animals.

tyrannosaurid
A tyrannosaurid is any member of the family Tyrannosauridae. This group, which includes albertosaurines and tyrannosaurines, is made up mainly of giant tyrannosaurs that lived during the latter half of the Cretaceous period. Tyrannosaurids are a type of tyrannosauroid.

tyrannosaurine
A tyrannosaurine is any member of the subfamily Tyrannosaurinae. The group includes not only tyrannosaurids that were close relatives of *T. rex* but also *T. rex* itself.

tyrannosauroid
A tyrannosauroid is any member of the superfamily Tyrannosauroidea. The group includes all tyrannosaurs.

Resources

Books
Barrett, P. *National Geographic Dinosaurs.* National Geographic Society, 2001.
Holtz, T. R., Jr., and L. V. Rey. *Dinosaurs: The Most Complete, Up-to-Date Encyclopedia for Dinosaur Lovers of All Ages.* Random House Books for Young Readers, 2007.
Lessem, D. *National Geographic Kids The Ultimate Dinopedia.* National Geographic Society, 2010.
Sloan, C. *Bizarre Dinosaurs: Some Very Strange Creatures and Why We Think They Got That Way.* National Geographic Children's Books, 2008.
Sloan, C. *Feathered Dinosaurs.* National Geographic Children's Books, 2000.
Sloan, C. *How Dinosaurs Took Flight: The Fossils, the Science, What We Think We Know, and Mysteries Yet Unsolved.* National Geographic Children's Books, 2005.

Websites/Online Resources
Learn all the facts and fun behind becoming a paleontologist and digging for dinosaurs.
www.amnh.org/explore/ology/paleontology

Check out dino info, a virtual dino dig, and a game.
paleobiology.si.edu/dinosaurs/interactives/dig/main.html

The University of California Museum of Paleontology is a reliable source for information about the history of life, facts about evolution, and geologic time.
www.ucmp.berkeley.edu/exhibits/index.php

Credits

All artwork by Xing Lida and Liu Yi unless otherwise noted. All graphics and maps by Science Visualization unless otherwise noted. P. 4, Ira Block/National Geographic Stock; p. 5, top: Hailong Zang/IVPP; bottom: Eva Koppelhus; p. 8, public domain; p. 9, Robert Clark/National Geographic Stock; p. 23, Xu Xing/IVPP; p. 25, Lindsay Zanno; p. 38, Christopher Sloan; p. 39, James Clark; pp. 40–41, Witmer Lab at Ohio University; p. 42, Raúl Martin/National Geographic Stock; p. 43, Greg Dale/National Geographic Stock; p. 44, IVPP; p. 45, Lars Grant-West/National Geographic Stock.

INDEX